The Special Stories Series
The Lost Puppy

by **KATE GAYNOR**

illustrated by **DONAL MANGAN**

Text copyright © Kate Gaynor, 2008

Illustrations copyright © Donal Mangan, 2008

All rights reserved. No part of this publication may be reproduced, stored in or introduced into a
retrieval system, or transmitted in any form or by any means (electronic, mechanical,
photocopying, recording or otherwise) without the prior written permission of both
the owner of the copyright and the publisher of this book.

The names, characters and incidents portrayed in all these works are fictitious. Any resemblance to real persons,
living or dead is purely coincidental.

Published in 2008 by

SPECIAL STORIES PUBLISHING

Member of CLÉ – The Irish Book Publishers Association

ISBN 978-0-9555787-2-4

A catalogue record for this book is available from the British Library

Printed by

BELVEDERE PRINT LTD. DUBLIN, IRELAND

Special Stories Publishing

www.specialstories.net

Acknowledgements

Many thanks to Kieran, my father Michael, my brother George and my extended family and friends. Special thanks too to my uncle Liam Gaynor, Liz O'Donoghue, Eva Byrne and the Louth County Enterprise Board for all their endless encouragement, support and invaluable advice.

Special thanks to Aghna Hennigan and Leah O'Toole Enable Ireland Disability Services Ltd, Ballycoolin Rd, Dublin.

Special thanks also to Dr. Gerard Molloy Ph.D C.Psychol. whose time and effort with this project was so greatly appreciated.

About the Illustrator

Donal Mangan is currently studying Animation in Dun Laoghaire Institute of Art, Design and Technology. This is Donal's first delve into the world of children's book illustration. In the future, he hopes to write and illustrate his own books aswell as pursuing a career in Animation.

To read more about the special stories collection, visit the Special Stories website at:
www.specialstories.net

Kate Gaynor

for Kieran

Hi! my name is **Charlie**. I am five years old.

My favourite game is 'pass the ball' and my favourite animal is a big dog called Bonnie who lives in my house.

Even though I'm the same as every other little boy and girl, my legs are just not as strong as everyone else's.

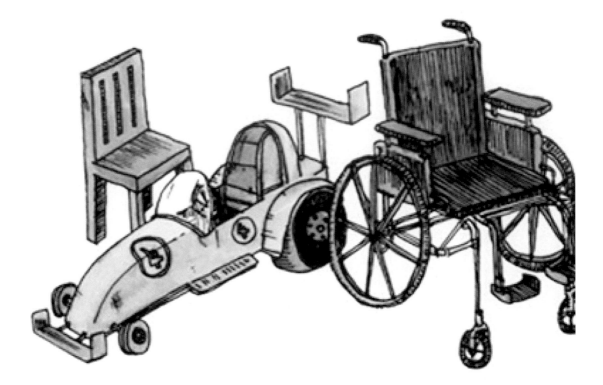

To help me, I use a special kind of chair called a wheelchair. It's exactly like a chair you sit on at the dinner table except it has wheels like a racing car, so they call it a wheelchair.

There are lots of different reasons why a boy or girl might need to use a wheelchair. Wheelchairs can help you move from place to place when your legs are just not able to carry you.

I used to think that having a wheelchair was hard work. You can't always go to the places that your friends do or play the games that you want to.

But then one day something happened that made me change my mind!

It was a hot, sunny day last summer when my friends and I decided to play a game of 'pass the ball' in the shade of a tree in the forest near my house.

The forest is home to a lot of animals and creatures. Sometimes when you hear a rustle in the bushes a colourful bird might fly out or sometimes it might be a rabbit or a hedgehog.

As we were playing our favourite game we heard something unusual rustling in the bushes. It sounded like crying.

We searched through the bushes and around the trees until finally we found where the sound was coming from.

ST. MARY'S UNIVERSITY COLLEGE

A COLLEGE OF THE QUEEN'S UNIVERSITY OF BELFAST

11

A tiny puppy had lost her way in the forest. She was caught in a trap and had hurt her leg.

My friend Liz wrapped the puppy's leg with a piece of cloth and we all wondered how we were going to carry her home.

When my friend Jim tried to lift her and put her over his shoulder she yelped and cried with pain. "I know" said my friend Pat, "I'll go back and get help".

But there was no time. The puppy was in a lot of pain from her injured leg and she needed to get to the vet straight away.

"What if I took her home on my knee?" I asked. "She'll be safe in my wheelchair and we won't hurt her injured leg".

The rest of my friends agreed and lifted the tiny puppy gently onto my lap. She rested there happily the whole way back to my house where the vet was waiting.

The vet told us that the puppy's leg was broken and gently bandaged it. He told me that even though Bonnie was the same as every other little dog; from now on her legs might not be just as strong.

18

"Just like me!" I said. "Yes!" said the vet, "so now a very brave dog can belong to an even braver boy, that's you!"

So what about you? Do you have a special story like mine? Why
don't you tell me all about it on your Special Story Page?

Your Special Story Page

Notes for Grown Up's for Children with Limited Mobility

There are a broad variety of reasons why young children become wheelchair users. From physical conditions like spina bifida, cerebral palsy and muscular dystrophy to spinal injuries caused by an accident or a fall.

Spina Bifida: There are many different forms of Spina Bifida but all result from incomplete development of the spine. The severity of this condition depends on the location of the split in the spinal cord. This is why some children born with spina bifida can walk and others cannot.

Cerebral Palsy: Cerebral palsy is not just one specific condition. It is used to refer to a large group of problems that can affect muscles, resulting in problems with body movement. Cerebral palsy can lead to weakness and lack of co-ordination of the muscles.

Muscular Dystrophy: Muscular dystrophy is the collective name for a range of neuromuscular conditions, which are characterized by the progressive weakening of the muscles. It can affect both adults and children. Some forms arise at birth or in childhood, others may not manifest themselves until later in life.

How to use this book

Children with limited mobility may often feel isolated from their peers as a result of being a wheelchair user. Through the experience of the main character, this book encourages children to look at their wheelchair as playing a positive rather than a negative role in their life. By reading this story with a young child, it also gives parents an opportunity to discuss any feelings of anxiety that their child may be feeling.

For information on disability in the Republic of Ireland please contact Enable Ireland at **www.enableireland.ie** *or* **+ 353 (0)1 872 7155**.

Enable Ireland
Action on Disability

For information outside Ireland please contact your local disability association.

Kate Gaynor

Other books from Special Stories Publishing

A FAMILY FOR SAMMY: The purpose of this book is to help explain the foster care process to young children.

JOE'S SPECIAL STORY: This story was written to help explain inter-country adoption to young children.

FIRST PLACE: The aim of this book is to help children to understand and accept the effects of cleft palate, cleft lip or any speech impediment in their lives and most importantly, how best to overcome them.

THE WINNER: The intention of this book is to help explain Asthma and its effects to young children.

THE BRAVEST GIRL IN SCHOOL: The objective of this story is to help children with diabetes to appreciate the importance of taking their insulin injections and being aware of what they eat.

THE FAMOUS HAT: The goal of this book is to help children with leukaemia (or other forms of cancer) to prepare for treatment, namely chemotherapy, and a stay in hospital.

To read more about the special stories collection, visit the Special Stories website at:
www.specialstories.net